I0559057

Son of Man

The Glory Hidden in Flesh

A Journey Through the Mystery of
Yeshua's Most Mysterious Name

DAMIANO B. CENTOLA

EXPLORA BOOKS
700 – 838 West Hastings St. Vancouver
BC V6C 0A6
www.explorabooks.com
Phone: (604) 330 6795

No part of this book may be reproduced, stored in a retrieval system, or transmitted by any means without the written permission of the author.

Because of the dynamic nature of the Internet, any web addresses or links contained in this book may have changed since publication and may no longer be valid. The views expressed in this work are solely those of the author and do not necessarily reflect the views of the publisher, and the publisher hereby disclaims any responsibility for them.

Bible verses are quoted from the King James Version (KJV), which is public domain, the English Standard Version (ESV), and the New King James Version (NKJV).

ISBN: 978-1-997587-78-1 (*Paperback*)
978-1-83430-042-9 (*Hardback*)
978-1-83430-043-6 (*eBook*)

© 2025 Damiano B. Centola. All rights reserved.

Son of Man

TABLE OF CONTENTS

CHAPTER 1
One Like a Son of Man
The Hidden Glory in Daniel's Vision 1

CHAPTER 2
The Name He Chose Most Unveiling
the Hidden Glory in Jesus 'Most Frequent Self-Title 5

CHAPTER 3
The Second Adam The Son of Man
Who Reverses the Curse...11

CHAPTER 4
Heaven's Ladder The Son of Man
Who Reconnects Earth and God...17

CHAPTER 5
The Suffering Servant The Son of Man Who Bore Our Sorrows........23

CHAPTER 6
The Coming Judge The Son of Man
Who Will Judge the Nations 31

CHAPTER 7
The Bread from Heaven The Son of Man
Who Nourishes Eternal Life..37

CHAPTER 8
The Veil of Flesh The Son of Man
Who Conceals Glory in Humanity..43

CHAPTER 9
The Return on the Clouds The Son of Man
Who Comes in Power and Glory 49

CHAPTER 10
Dominion Restored The Son of Man
Who Reclaims What Was Lost 55

CHAPTER 11
The Suffering Son of Man
The Wounds That Prove His Glory 61

CHAPTER 12
The Son of Man and the Final Judgment
When Mercy Sits on the Throne 67

CHAPTER 13
The Glory Revealed in a Human Face Behold, the Man......................73

CHAPTER 14
The Son of Man in Us Glory Reflected Through Dust.........................79

CHAPTER 15
Epilogue: When the Son of Man Stands 85

ACKNOWLEDGMENTS 91
ABOUT THE AUTHOR..97
Other Books by Damiano B. Centola.......................................93
REFERENCES & SOURCE CITATIONS 95

This is the Son of Man—
the Glory hidden in flesh,
the Fire wrapped in dust,
the Mirror of God restored.

THE FACE OF DUST AND GLORY

Dunuano B. Centola

Hic est Filius Hominis—
Gloria in carne abscondita,
Ignis pulvere tectus
Speculum Dei restitutum
nta l'acqua ca torna puru pulita.

SON OF MAN
THE GLORY HIDDEN IN FLESH

1 **Veiled in Humanity** Philippians 2.6 Jesus veils divinity in humanity	**2** **The Exalted Redeemer** Daniel 7:15-14 Eternal dominion from the Ancient of Days	**3** **The Last Adam** 1 Corinthians 15:45 Jesus as the new head of redeemed humanity
4 **Ladder Between Heaven and Earth** John 1:51 / Genesis 25 Jesus is the divine connection between heaven and earth	**5** **Suffering and Rejection** Isaiah 53 Mak 8³¹ Messiah's glory through suffering and rejection	**6** **Revelation and Judgment** Marthew 25:31 Final judgment by glorified Son of Man
7 **The Bread of Life** John 6.53 Jesus gives His flesh and blood for eternal life	**8** **Majesty Through Humility** Philippians 2.5-11 Divine majesty revealed through humility	**9** **Dust Made Holy** Hebrews 2.14 He redeems dust and enthrones humanity

Image of the Invisible	Image of the Invisible

CHAPTER 1
One Like a Son of Man
The Hidden Glory in Daniel's Vision

Before He walked on water, before He healed the blind, before He was wrapped in swaddling cloth in Bethlehem.

He was seen—in a vision.

A prophet in exile, far from home, trembling under the weight of Babylon's beasts, was shown a throne.

Not of men.

Not of corruption.

But of the Ancient of Days, aflame with fire, surrounded by countless witnesses, and upon it came one like the Son of Man.

The Scene in Daniel 7

The setting is apocalyptic. Empires are rising and falling, represented by monstrous beasts: a lion, a bear, a leopard, and a terrifying creature with iron teeth and ten horns. These are earthly powers—kingdoms that devour, manipulate, and trample.

But then the vision shifts.

*"I saw in the night visions, and, behold, one like the
Son of Man came with the clouds of heaven, and
came to the Ancient of Days, and they brought Him
near before Him. And there was given Him
dominion, and glory, and a kingdom, that all
people, nations, and languages, should serve Him..."*

— Daniel 7:13–14 (KJV)

This is not just a hopeful human.

This is a divine figure—one who comes on the clouds, a description used only for God in the Old Testament Psalm 104:3; Nahum 1:3). In Hebrew thought, riding the clouds was reserved for YHWH alone. And yet here is "One like a Son of Man"—a human form, but bearing divine prerogative. This was not a mere metaphor. To Daniel, it was a mystery. A human figure exalted in the heavens. A man standing in the place of God, receiving authority, worship, and eternal dominion from the Ancient of Days Himself.

This passage—Daniel 7:13–14—would become the theological nucleus of Jesus self-understanding. In a single, explosive vision, we are introduced to the paradox that Jesus would later embody:

"The One who comes down like dust...
is the One who ascends with clouds."

Why It Matters

Daniel's vision is not background noise. It's not apocalyptic filler. It is the cornerstone of the most repeated title Jesus used for Himself: Son of Man. When Jesus stood before the Sanhedrin at His trial, He was silent for most of the accusations. But when asked if He was the Messiah, the Son of God, He responded:

"You will see the Son of Man seated at the right
hand of Power, and coming with the clouds of
heaven."

— Mark 14:62 (ESV)

They tore their garments not just because He claimed to be the Messiah, but because He claimed Daniel 7—a passage reserved for divine authority. In that moment, Jesus was saying:

I am the human who reigns like God,

and the God who has become human.

The Meaning of "Like a Son of Man"

The phrase "like a son of man" in Aramaic (kebar enash) means a human-like figure—not a beast, not an angel, but one who shares our frame, our fragility. This language draws a direct contrast with the inhuman empires of Daniel 7: the beasts that claw and crush.

Where the kingdoms of men dehumanize, this Man restores humanity. Where the empires devour, this Man offers bread.

Where the rulers of the earth demand worship, this Man receives it because He is worthy. Daniel's vision is not just prophecy—it is apocalyptic anthropology: it redefines what it means to be human in the light of divine glory. The beasts become less than human. The Son of Man becomes more than human.

Jesus and the Return to Daniel

Why did Jesus so frequently call Himself the Son of Man? He was anchoring His identity in Daniel 7. But here's the shock: instead of claiming the glory of Daniel's vision first, He claimed the suffering that would precede it.

> *"The Son of Man must suffer many things... and be killed, and after three days rise again."*
>
> *— Mark 8:31*

In effect, Jesus rewrites expectations:

- Daniel saw the Son of Man in glory,
- Jesus became the Son of Man in agony, so that when He comes in glory again, He will come not to crush, but to redeem.

Dominion, But Not Yet

When Jesus rose from the dead and ascended into heaven, He did not claim a throne of violence. He claimed a kingdom of hearts, a dominion of grace, and a people formed not by swords, but by Spirit.
The fulfillment of Daniel 7 was begun in resurrection,
but it will be consummated in the return.
This is why He says in Matthew 24:30:

> *"Then shall appear the sign of the Son of Man in heaven... and they shall see the Son of Man coming in the clouds of heaven with power and great glory."*

He has not abandoned Daniel's vision. He is building toward it—brick by brick, soul by soul, generation by generation.

A Final Word

The beasts are still among us—empires that dehumanize, leaders that devour, systems that silence the image of God in man.
But the Son of Man has already come.
And He will come again.
When He does, He will not come as a beast, but as a man radiant with glory, full of mercy, crowned in majesty, and holding dominion not by terror but by truth.

Until that day, we live between the verses:

- Between Daniel's vision and its final fulfillment,
- Between a manger and the clouds,
- Between the cross and the throne.

We live as those who follow the Son of Man.

And in following Him, we find not only who He is we find who we are meant to be.

CHAPTER 2
The Name He Chose Most Unveiling the
Hidden Glory in Jesus Most Frequent Self-Title

It was not "King of Kings."

It was not "Messiah."

It was not even "Son of God."

Of all the titles available to Him—royal, prophetic, divine—Yeshua most often referred to Himself as "the Son of Man."

More than eighty times in the Gospels, this phrase falls from His lips like a signature written across His mission. Quietly. Deliberately. Without fanfare.

This chapter will explore why.

Why did Jesus, the Lord of Glory, choose a name that sounds so ordinary—so human?

And why has this name remained so mysterious to most readers, even two thousand years later?

A Name That Hides and Reveals

To call Himself Son of Man was, in many ways, an act of concealment. At first glance, the phrase seems humble—maybe even vague. It's not a title that shouts divinity. It doesn't glow with celestial light or stir prophetic imagination. To some ears, it may have sounded like a way of saying, "I am just a man."

But herein lies the genius—and the mystery.

"Son of Man" is the title that hides divine glory
inside human language."

It is a veil, and a window.

A paradox in three words.

A title that descends lower than angels, and then rises to the right hand of the Father. It's not a retreat from His identity.

It is the slow unfolding of it.

The Gospel Records: A Pattern of Self-Identification

Let's observe the Gospels.

In Matthew, Mark, Luke, and John, Jesus consistently refers to Himself as the Son of Man—not a son of man, but the. This distinction matters. He's not identifying as one of many humans. He's claiming a unique role, a specific destiny, a divine mystery wrapped in human form.

He says:

- "The Son of Man has authority on earth to forgive sins." (Mark 2:10)
- "The Son of Man is Lord even of the Sabbath." (Mark 2:28)
- "The Son of Man came not to be served but to serve, and to give His life as a ransom for many." (Mark 10:45)
- "You will see the Son of Man seated at the right hand of Power and coming on the clouds of heaven." (Mark 14:62)

From forgiveness to authority, from servanthood to divine enthronement—Jesus loads this title with staggering meaning.

He stretches the name "Son of Man" to cover the full arc of His mission: incarnation, crucifixion, resurrection, ascension, and return.

This is not mere humility.

This is heaven disguised in humility.

Not an Invention of the Gospels

Critics have argued that perhaps the "Son of Man" language was added later by Gospel writers to shape Jesus into a more approachable figure. But this doesn't hold up to close examination.

If the early church were inventing a divine figure, they would've leaned more heavily on "Son of God", "Christ", or "Lord"—titles already familiar in Greco-Roman and Jewish culture. Instead, the evangelists preserve Jesus 'own vocabulary, even when it confuses readers or complicates the narrative.

Why? Because it's true. Because it's what He called Himself.

This was not an editorial gloss—it was a living mystery.

The Gospel of John, considered the most theologically reflective of the four, begins with "the Word was God" but preserves "Son of Man" repeatedly:

"No one has ascended into heaven except He who descended from heaven, the Son of Man."

(John 3:13)

"Do not labor for the food that perishes, but for the food that endures to eternal life, which the Son of Man will give to you."

(John 6:27)

The very same Jesus who is called the Logos, the Lamb of God, the Bread of Life, still calls Himself. "Son of Man."

Because only this name—this paradox of dust and divinity—could carry the full weight of what He came to do.

Hidden in the Prophets, Revealed in the Flesh

We must also understand that "Son of Man" is not a New Testament innovation.

It is a phrase deeply embedded in the Jewish Scriptures.

- In Ezekiel, God calls the prophet "son of man" nearly 90 times, underscoring human frailty in contrast to divine power. It was a way of saying:

"You are not God. You are dust. Speak, but know your place."

- In Daniel, however, the phrase explodes into glory. As we explored in Chapter 1, Daniel sees "one like a son of man" coming on the clouds, receiving eternal dominion and worship. This figure is both human and more than human—a being who enters the throne room of the Ancient of Days and receives a kingdom that will never be destroyed.

When Jesus uses this title, He is not simply identifying with human weakness (like in Ezekiel). He is claiming the exalted figure of Daniel 7, while embodying the suffering figure of Isaiah 53.

In other words:

- He is the Son of Man who bleeds.
- He is the Son of Man who reigns.
- He is the Son of Man who bridges dust and glory.

Why He Didn't Call Himself "Son of God"

Jesus is indeed the Son of God—eternally begotten, not made. And the Gospels affirm this truth from beginning to end.

But He rarely uses that title for Himself. Why?

Because the phrase "Son of God," especially in Roman times, could be easily misunderstood.

Caesars called themselves "sons of the gods." Kings claimed divine status. The term had been diluted by politics, mythology, and pride.

But Son of Man? That phrase was loaded with mystery—misunderstood by some, but never co-opted by empires. It allowed Jesus to redefine kingship on His terms, not theirs.

He would not come as Caesar.

He would come as the Servant-King.

And the Son of Man was the perfect title for such a mission.

It was a name no one else dared to wear.

And yet it was a name only He could truly fulfill.

A Title for the Beginning, the Middle, and the End

The first time He preaches, He uses it.

The last time He speaks before the cross, He uses it.

At His return, He promises it will be the name the world sees when He comes again.

No other title weaves its way through every moment of His ministry like Son of Man.

It is the name for:

- His humility: "Foxes have holes... but the Son of Man has nowhere to lay His head."
- His mission: "The Son of Man came to seek and save the lost."
- His authority: "The Son of Man has power on earth to forgive sins."
- His suffering: "The Son of Man must suffer, be rejected... and rise again."
- His future: "You will see the Son of Man coming on the clouds."

What It Means for Us

By choosing this name, Jesus does more than describe Himself—
He redefines what it means to be human.
The Son of Man is not a distant deity.
He is not wrapped in philosophical abstraction or imperial power.
He is close enough to touch, but holy enough to worship.
In Him, we learn that being human is not a limitation to be despised, but a vessel through which God chooses to dwell.
The Son of Man shows us:

- That it's possible to walk in weakness and yet carry glory.
- That humility does not hide power—it reveals its true form.
- That the dust of our frame was never beneath God's touch.
- That to be human, rightly lived, is to be holy.

A Final Reflection

He could have called Himself by a hundred names.
He could have worn heaven like a crown.
But He chose this title—not because He needed to descend, but because we needed Him to.
And now, through Him, we are no longer just sons and daughters of Adam.
We are being remade in the image of the Son of Man.
He is not ashamed to call us brethren.
And we are not afraid to call Him ours.

CHAPTER 3
The Second Adam
The Son of Man Who Reverses the Curse

He stooped down, not into sin, but into flesh.

He stepped not away from glory, but into dust.

And when He rose, He did not just rise as one man—He rose as a new humanity.

To understand why Jesus is called the Son of Man, we must not only look forward to His dominion in glory, but backward to Eden, where humanity was first formed—and where it first fell.

The Apostle Paul calls Jesus "the last Adam" (1 Corinthians 15:45), and through this lens we begin to see the full weight of the title Son of Man. It is not just a reference to His humanity. It is a statement of new creation. He is not just one of us—He is the reset of us.

Adam: The Son of Dust

In Genesis 2:7, the LORD God forms man from the dust of the earth and breathes into his nostrils the breath of life. Adam becomes the living image of God—earth formed by heaven, dust charged with glory.

But it doesn't last.

The man who was formed in the image of God chooses to grasp for something more.

He forgets he was made in divine likeness and reaches for godhood on his own terms.

In doing so, Adam falls—not just as a man, but as mankind's head.

From Adam's sin comes death.

From Adam's rebellion comes separation.

From Adam's choice, the world breaks.

And every man after Adam bears his dust, his weakness, his wound.

Jesus Enters the Line of Adam

When Jesus calls Himself the Son of Man, He is identifying with the fallen race of Adam—but not to repeat the story.
He has come to rewrite it.
In Luke's genealogy, the line of Jesus is traced not merely to Abraham, but all the way to Adam, "the son of God" (Luke 3:38). This is intentional. It places Jesus in the same human stream—not above it, not beside it—but within it.
But where Adam failed in a garden, Jesus would overcome in one.
Where Adam was tempted and fell, Jesus would be tempted and stand.
Where Adam brought death, Jesus would bring life.
He enters not just as a Savior, but as the new head of a new humanity.

The Wilderness Test
In Matthew 4, Jesus is led by the Spirit into the wilderness to be tempted.
This is not incidental. This is a reenactment of Eden, but under far harsher conditions.
Adam was tempted in a garden of abundance.
Jesus is tempted in a wilderness of lack.
Adam had companionship.
Jesus is alone.
Adam was surrounded by beauty.
Jesus is surrounded by desolation.
And still—Jesus stands.
Where Adam listens to the serpent's voice, Jesus silences him with the Word of God.
This is not just moral victory—it is covenantal reversal.
He is undoing Adam's disobedience through His obedience.

The Garden Revisited

Later, in Gethsemane, the Second Adam faces a deeper test.

> *"Father, if it be possible, let this cup pass from me.*
> *Nevertheless, not as I will, but as thou wilt."*

> — *Matthew 26:39*

This moment echoes Eden—but with a different outcome.
In the first garden, Adam says:

> *"Not Thy will, but mine be done."*

In the second garden, Jesus says:

> *"Not My will, but Thine be done."*

The curse began with rebellion in a garden.
Redemption begins with surrender in a garden.

The Breath Recovered

In Genesis, God breathes into Adam, and he becomes a living soul.
In John 20:22, the resurrected Jesus breathes on His disciples, saying:

> *"Receive the Holy Spirit."*

This is not just symbolism—it is creation language.
It is the second breath of God into man.
What was lost in Adam's disobedience is restored in
Christ's resurrection.
Jesus, the Son of Man, breathes not mere oxygen—but Spirit.
He is not just alive—He is life-giving.

Paul's Theology of the Two Adams

In Romans 5, Paul lays it out with stunning clarity:

> *"For as by one man's disobedience many were made*
> *sinners, so by the obedience of one shall many be*
> *made righteous."*

> — *Romans 5:19*

And again, in 1 Corinthians 15:

> *"The first man Adam was made a living soul; the*
> *last Adam was made a quickening spirit."*

> *— 1 Corinthians 15:45*

This is the heart of the Gospel. Jesus did not just die to forgive sins.
He came to inaugurate a new humanity.
In Him, we don't just receive pardon—we receive a new nature.
The Son of Man becomes the beginning of a new race,
one that reflects not the image of dust, but the image of the heavenly.

The Resurrected Man

Jesus rises from the grave still bearing the title Son of Man. He is not a ghost.
He is flesh renewed, wounds glorified, body transfigured.
He eats with His disciples.
He shows them His scars.
He walks and talks and ascends—not as an idea, but as a Man.
These matters.
Because if He rose as God only, then humanity remains buried.
But if He rose as Son of Man, then humanity is lifted.
And so, Paul writes:

> *"As we have borne the image of the man of dust, we*
> *shall also bear the image of the man of heaven."*

> *— 1 Corinthians 15:49*

What It Means for Us

We were born in Adam. We inherited his loss.
But now, in Christ, we inherit His life.
This is not poetic metaphor.
It is ontological transformation.
To be "in Christ" is not merely to follow a teacher.
It is to be grafted into a new humanity,
to be made new not just in destiny, but in nature.

Through the Son of Man:

- Dust is not discarded—it is redeemed.
- Flesh is not condemned—it is glorified.
- Humanity is not bypassed—it is rebuilt from within.

Jesus does not erase Adam—He replaces him.

Final Reflection: From Earth to Heaven

In the end, the story of the Second Adam is not just about one Man.
It's about all who follow Him.
Through Him, we pass from:

- Condemnation to righteousness,
- Corruption to incorruption,
- Mortality to immortality.

And so, the Son of Man becomes not only our Savior,
but our source, our head, our hope.
He is the blueprint.
He is the breath.
He is the first of many.
The Second Adam has stood where the first fell.
And because of Him,
the children of dust will rise with the glory of the heavens.

THE SON ON MAN AND THE HUMAN FRAME

A Diagram of Divine Geometry, Breath, and Glory

DAMIANO B. CENTOLA

CHAPTER 4
Heaven's Ladder
The Son of Man Who Reconnects Earth and God

There is a ladder set up in the dark.

Not built by men.

Not fashioned by religion.

Not climbed by effort.

It descends from the heavens and rests on the earth, not in a temple, but in a field—not in a king's court, but beside a wandering, broken man.

In Genesis 28, the patriarch Jacob lies on the hard ground, using a stone for a pillow. He is not noble in this moment. He has deceived his father, betrayed his brother, and fled in shame. Alone, guilty, and unsure of his future, he falls asleep under the stars.

And in that place—God meets him.

> *"And he dreamed, and behold a ladder set up on the*
> *earth, and the top of it reached to heaven: and*
> *behold the angels of God ascending and descending*
> *on it."*

> *— Genesis 28:12*

He wakes in awe and says:

> *"Surely the Lord is in this place; and I knew it not."*

> *— Genesis 28:16*

That vision would live in Jewish memory for centuries—an image of divine connection, of God stooping low, of heaven reaching earth. But it would remain a mystery, a symbol—until Jesus stood before Nathanael and said:

> *"Truly, truly, I say to you, you will see heaven*
> *opened, and the angels of God ascending and*
> *descending upon the Son of Man."— John 1:51*

In that moment, the ladder had a name.

Jesus is the ladder.

The Son of Man is the staircase between God and man.

The First Bridge Was Broken

In Eden, there was no separation between God and man.

Adam walked with the Lord in the cool of the day.

There was no need for a ladder.

Heaven and earth were aligned—intimate, interwoven, inseparable.

But sin shattered that union.

And the story of Scripture is the story of God's effort to reconnect what was lost.

Throughout the Old Testament, we see echoes of this divine descent:

- A burning bush in the wilderness.
- A cloud over Sinai.
- The ark of the covenant between cherubim.
- A temple filled with glory.

But all of these were temporary shadows—provisional bridges.

Then, at last, came the true connection—a Person, not a place.

A Man who is both God and human.

A Body that spans both heaven and earth.

Jesus, the Son of Man, is not just the messenger—He is the meeting point.

Jacob's Vision Fulfilled

When Jacob saw the ladder, it was a mystery.

When Jesus referenced the ladder, it was a revelation.

He was telling Nathanael—and all who would hear:

> *"That ladder your ancestors dreamed of? The connection they longed for? The divine-human meeting place? It's Me."*

Not metaphor. Not allegory.

Literal spiritual architecture.

The ladder is not something we climb to reach God.

It is something God descended to reach us.

And He did it by putting on flesh.

Heaven Opened

Throughout the Gospels, Jesus speaks of heaven being opened.
It's a repeated phrase with profound meaning:

- At His baptism: "The heavens were opened, and the Spirit descended like a dove."
- Before Nathanael: "You will see heaven opened."
- In Revelation: "I saw heaven opened, and behold, a white horse…"

This image of the opened heavens is more than just dramatic scenery.
It is the undoing of separation.
It is the veil torn.
The judgment lifted.
The distance closed.
Jesus is the One through whom the heavens are permanently opened.
In Him, the gates of glory no longer swing shut behind priests
and prophets.
They are flung open for tax collectors, fishermen, and children.
For the poor in spirit.
For the pure in heart.
For all who believe.
The Meaning of "Son of Man" in John 1:51
It's significant that when Jesus speaks of the angels ascending and
descending, He says they do so upon the Son of Man.
He does not say through Me or around Me.
He says on Me.
In Jewish tradition, angels ascending and descending meant divine
activity—messages going up, power coming down, the unseen working
among the seen.
But now, all of that is happening on the Son of Man.
He becomes the place where prayer and answer meet.
Where sin and mercy collide.
Where death and life intersect.
He is the living ladder—the Son of Man who stands between the Father
and the world, lifting us by His intercession, carrying us by His cross,
raising us by His resurrection.

A Better Bethel

Jacob named the place of his vision Bethel, meaning "house of God."
But Jesus later declares:

"Destroy this temple, and in three days I will raise it up."

— John 2:19

He wasn't speaking of stones.
He was speaking of His body.
He is the true Bethel.
The house of God is not made with hands.
It is made with flesh and Spirit.
The Son of Man is the meeting place now.
You do not need to go to a mountain or a sanctuary.
You need only come to Him.

When the Ladder Descended Lower

We might think the incarnation was the lowest rung of the ladder.
But it went lower.
Jesus—eternally divine—descends into human form.
Then into servant form.
Then into suffering.
Then into death.
Then into burial.
This is the ladder going beneath the earth, so that even there, in the grave, God might reach the lost.
There is no rung too low for the Son of Man.

What It Means for Us

Every religion offers a ladder.
Do this.
Pray that.
Climb higher.
Ascend by works, by rituals, by knowledge, by sacrifice.
But only one offers a descending ladder.

Only one says:

"You can't climb to Me—so I came down to you."

2To believe in Jesus as the Son of Man is to believe:

- That heaven has already touched earth.
- That we don't strive upward—we receive downward.
- That union with God is not achieved, but given.

And more:

The Son of Man is not just the ladder we receive—He is the ladder we become.

In Him, we too become living connections between heaven and earth.

We become temples of the Spirit.

We carry the divine into the ordinary.

As He is, so we are.

A Final Reflection

In a world where the heavens often feel silent

where prayers rise and answers delay—we remember the ladder.

It is not just an ancient dream.

It is a living reality.

There is a ladder set up in the dark.

It has a name.

It has scars.

It walks among us still.

And upon it, angels still ascend and descend.

Still move.

Still respond.

Because Jesus, the Son of Man, is not just the bridge.

He is the God who crosses it.

CHAPTER 5
The Suffering Servant
The Son of Man Who Bore Our Sorrows

There are titles that announce strength.

There are names that evoke majesty.

But some names whisper through blood, through silence, through bruises and betrayal.

And among those, none speaks more softly—

and more powerfully—than "the Son of Man must suffer."

This was not what Israel expected.

This was not what the world was looking for.

The one who would sit on David's throne, who would rule the nations with a rod of iron—He must suffer?

He must be rejected?

He must die?

Yes.

Because glory does not rise from gold, but from graveyards.

And the Son of Man came not first to reign—but to bleed.

The Turning Point in the Gospels

The Gospels are structured with intentional design.

In each of the Synoptics—Matthew, Mark, and Luke—there is a pivotal moment where Jesus begins to speak plainly about His suffering.

It follows Peter's confession at Caesarea Philippi:

> *"You are the Christ, the Son of the Living God."*

> *— Matthew 16:16*

And immediately after:

> *"From that time forth began Jesus to show unto His disciples, how that He must go unto Jerusalem, and suffer many things... and be killed, and be raised again the third day."*

> *— Matthew 16:21*

In Mark's Gospel, this is the first of three explicit predictions.
Each time, Jesus refers to Himself as the Son of Man:

- "The Son of Man must suffer many things…"
- "The Son of Man is delivered into the hands of men…"
- "The Son of Man shall be betrayed unto the chief priests…"

This repeated rhythm is intentional.
It is not simply about foretelling His death.
It is about redefining the title "Son of Man."
The One seen in Daniel's vision—robed in dominion, descending on clouds—He will first be robed in blood, crowned with thorns, and lifted not on clouds but on a cross.

Isaiah's Servant

Long before Jesus walked the dusty roads of Galilee, a prophet saw His shadow:

> *"He is despised and rejected of men; a man of sorrows, and acquainted with grief... He was wounded for our transgressions, He was bruised for our iniquities..."*

> *— Isaiah 53:3, 5*

This is not the Messiah of military strength.
This is not the conquering king of popular expectation.
This is the Servant.

- He does not strike back.
- He does not defend Himself.
- He is led like a lamb to slaughter, silent before His accusers.

And in His wounds, we find healing.
Jesus not only fulfills Isaiah's prophecy—He embodies it.
He does not just suffer with us.
He suffers for us.
And more—He suffers as us.

He takes the weight of sin.
The silence of shame.
The full fury of justice.
And He does so willingly.

The Scandal of a Crucified Messiah

To modern readers, the cross may feel familiar—even sacred.
But to the first-century world, it was scandalous.

> *"Cursed is everyone who hangs on a tree."*

> *— Deuteronomy 21:23*

To claim that the Son of Man would die such a death was to upend every expectation.
It was not just counterintuitive—it was offensive.
This is why Paul wrote:

> *"We preach Christ crucified: to the Jews a*
> *stumbling block, and to the Greeks foolishness."*

> *— 1 Corinthians 1:23*

But what was foolishness to men was wisdom to God.
In the crucified Son of Man, heaven is not embarrassed.
Heaven is enthroned.
The cross is not a detour.
It is the very road to glory.

The Necessity of Suffering

Jesus does not say the Son of Man may suffer.
He says He must.

> *"The Son of Man must suffer many things..."*

> *— Mark 8:31*

This "must" is the language of divine necessity.
Why?
Because justice must be satisfied.
Because sin must be atoned.
Because death must be destroyed from the inside out. And only One
who is truly human and truly holy can carry that weight.
The Son of Man becomes the suffering servant because no one
else can.

Gethsemane: The Garden of Crushing

The suffering reaches its crescendo in Gethsemane.

There, Jesus prays:

"My soul is exceeding sorrowful, even unto death."

— Matthew 26:38

He sweats blood.

He falls on His face.

He is not crushed by nails yet—but by grief, by anticipation, by the cup He must drink.

This is not staged drama.

This is a Man bearing the world's judgment before the whip ever touches His back.

And yet, in that place of agony, the Son of Man does not flinch.

He says, "Thy will be done."

In Gethsemane, the suffering servant does what Adam could not—He obeys.

The Mockery of Kingship

At the trial, Jesus is silent before false accusations.

At the scourging post, He is stripped and whipped.

At the crucifixion, they crown Him—not with gold, but with thorns.

The soldier's mock:

"Hail, King of the Jews!"

But heaven is watching.

Because this is the coronation of the Son of Man.

Not in power, but in pain.

Not on clouds, but on a cross.

Not with applause, but with blood.

And from that throne of wood, He rules by dying.

What It Means for Us

We follow a crucified Messiah.

- This means pain is not pointless.
- This means suffering can be redemptive.
- This means God does not avoid agony—He enters it.

The Son of Man teaches us:

- That wounds can be sacred.
- That weakness can be strength.
- That love is measured not by comfort, but by sacrifice.

And in our own sorrows, we find not only sympathy—but solidarity.

"Surely He has borne our griefs, and carried our sorrows…"

The Blood That Speaks

Hebrews tells us that Jesus 'blood speaks a better word than the blood of Abel.

Where Abel's blood cried for justice,

Jesus 'blood cries for mercy.

And as the Son of Man hangs between earth and sky, He bridges not just heaven and humanity—but the guilty and the forgiven, the dead and the living.

Final Reflection

When Jesus says, "The Son of Man must suffer,"

He is not withdrawing into sadness.

He is advancing toward glory.

Because from His wounds come rivers.

From His stripes come healing.

From His cross comes a kingdom.

And the One who suffers for us now reigns with scars—not erased, but exalted.

The Son of Man did not avoid pain.

He walked into it—so that we would never walk through it alone.

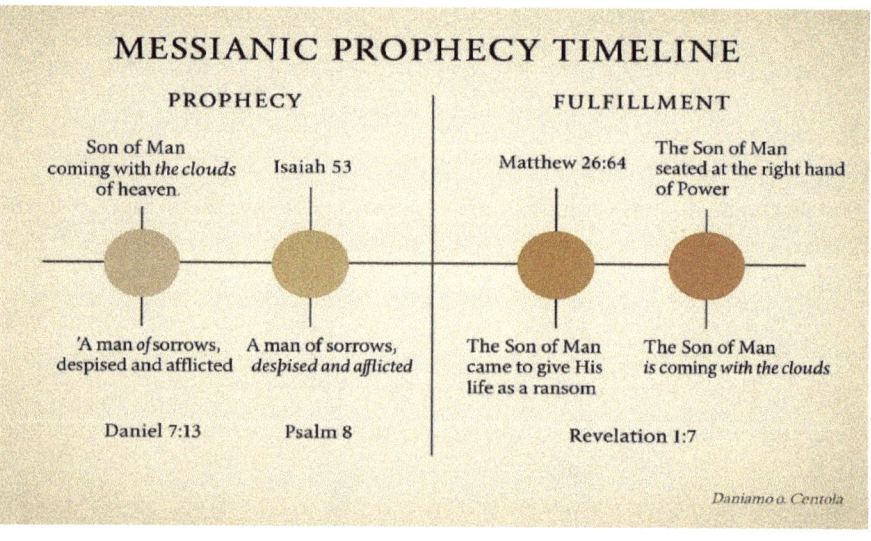

MESSIANIC PROPHECY TIMELINE

PROPHECY

FULFILLMENT

Son of Man coming with *the clouds* of heaven.

Isaiah 53

Matthew 26:64

The Son of Man seated at the right hand of Power

'A man *of* sorrows, despised and afflicted

A man of sorrows, *despised and afflicted*

The Son of Man came to give His life as a ransom

The Son of Man *is coming with the clouds*

Daniel 7:13

Psalm 8

Revelation 1:7

Daniamo o. Centola

From shadow to substance, from promise to Person — the arc of glory bends through time and finds its name in Yeshua.

D.B.C.

CHAPTER 6
The Coming Judge
The Son of Man Who Will Judge the Nations

He came in obscurity.

He came as a servant.

He came with pierced hands and dusty feet.

But He will return—not in silence, not in shame, but in glory.

The Son of Man, who once walked among fishermen and outcasts, will come again—on clouds, with power, with angels, and with fire.

And this time, He will not stand accused.

This time, He will judge.

From Suffering Servant to Sovereign Judge

There is a dramatic shift in how Jesus refers to Himself as the Son of Man between His first and second comings.

- In His first coming, the title Son of Man emphasized humility, incarnation, and suffering.
- But when He speaks of His return, it is the same title— but with unveiled majesty.

"When the Son of Man shall come in His glory, and
all the holy angels with Him, then shall He sit upon
the throne of His glory."

— Matthew 25:31

This is no longer the Son of Man in Gethsemane.

This is the Son of Man in Daniel 7, come full circle.

He is no longer veiling His dominion—He is executing it.

The Language of Glory

Notice the language Jesus uses:

- "All the angels with Him…"
- "He will sit on His glorious throne…"
- "Before Him will be gathered all nations…"

This is the language of cosmic judgment.

It's not regional. It's not symbolic.

It is universal and literal.

The Son of Man will not judge a courtroom—

He will judge the world.

And it will not be by opinion or reputation, but by truth.

Matthew 25: The Judgment of the Sheep and Goats

Perhaps the most well-known passage about the Son of Man's judgment is in Matthew 25. Here, Jesus describes a future day when He, as the Son of Man, sits on His throne and separates all people into two groups:

- The sheep, who inherit the kingdom.
- The goats, who are cast out.

What is the basis of this judgment?

"I was hungry and you gave Me food… I was a stranger and you welcomed Me…"

And when the righteous ask, "When did we see You like this?"

He replies:

"Inasmuch as you did it unto one of the least of these My brethren, you did it unto Me."

This is staggering.

The Son of Man is not judging based on rituals or knowledge, but on love.

Not by titles, but by actions toward the vulnerable.

Not by confession alone, but by compassion.

This is not salvation by works—but it is the proof of a transformed life.

What we do to others, Jesus counts as done to Himself.

John 5: Authority to Judge

In John's Gospel, Jesus makes the claim even more explicit:

"The Father judges no one, but has given all
judgment to the Son... and has given Him authority
to execute judgment, because He is the Son of Man."

— John 5:22, 27

Let that settle in:

The Father, who sits enthroned in eternity, has handed over the right to judge to His Son—not because He is God, but because He is the Son of Man.

This is profound.

Jesus judges the world not only as divine—but as human.

Because He knows what it is to walk this earth.

He knows temptation.

He knows injustice.

He knows the cost of mercy, the taste of sorrow.

Therefore, His judgment is perfect—not distant or detached, but personal, righteous, and true.

The Books Will Be Opened

In Revelation 20, we read of the great white throne:

"And I saw the dead, small and great, stand before
God; and the books were opened..."

The Son of Man will open the books.

Not just the books of history.

Not just the record of sin.

But the book of life.

And for those who are found in Him—

those who are washed in His blood—

there will be no condemnation.

Because the Judge has already paid the price.

The Paradox of the Judge with Scars

It is one thing to be judged by law.

It is another to be judged by love.

The Son of Man will come in glory—but He will still bear the scars.

The Judge is the Lamb.

The King is the Crucified.

And when He renders judgment, He does so not with glee, but with the heart of One who died to save those He must now sentence.
This is the paradox of divine justice:
The One who weeps over Jerusalem will also pronounce its fall.
The One who was mocked will silence every mouth.
The One who stood before Pilate will now summon kings to account.

What It Means for Us

The Son of Man as Judge is not a threat.
It is a warning, yes.
But more—it is a call to live honestly, compassionately, and ready.
Because:

- He sees. Nothing is hidden from Him.
- He remembers. Even a cup of cold water given in His name.
- He rewards. To the humble, the merciful, the faithful.

And He will come again.
Not in secret.
Not in silence.
But in splendor.

Living in Light of His Return

The early church lived with an urgency we have often forgotten.
They believed—rightly—that the Son of Man could return at
any moment.
This didn't make them fanatics.
It made them faithful.
They fed the poor.
They suffered with joy.
They laid down their lives, not to escape judgment—but because they had already passed from death into life.
We are called to live likewise.
Not in fear, but in holy readiness.

Final Reflection

The Son of Man will come again.
Not to teach.
Not to heal.
Not to be judged.
But to judge.
And when He does, it will not be a stranger on the throne—It will be the One who walked the earth.
The One who touched the leper.
The One who wept at the tomb.
The One who said, "Father, forgive them."
He is the Son of Man.
He is the Judge.
And He will be just.
But for those who know Him,
who love Him,
who have called on His name—the verdict has already been spoken:

> *"There is therefore now no condemnation to those*
> *who are in Christ Jesus."*

> *— Romans 8:1*

CHAPTER 7
The Bread from Heaven
The Son of Man Who Nourishes Eternal Life

The crowd had been fed, and their bellies were full.

Five thousand men, not counting women and children, had eaten from the hand of a miracle.

Barley loaves, a few fish—and yet more than enough.

They saw the sign. They tasted the bread.

But they misunderstood the Man.

They chased Him—not for who He was, but for what He could do.

And Jesus, knowing their hunger ran deeper than their stomachs, turned to them and said:

> *"Do not labor for the food that perishes, but for the*
> *food that endures to everlasting life, which the Son*
> *of Man will give you..."*
>
> *— John 6:27*

This is where the mystery deepens.

Because the One who fed them now speaks of Himself as the bread.

The One who multiplies provision reveals that He is the provision.

And the title He uses again?

The same name: Son of Man.

The Setting: Hunger Beyond the Flesh

John 6 is one of the most layered, mysterious, and theologically dense chapters in the New Testament. It is both miracle and mystery, nourishment and offense.

After the miracle of the loaves, the people pursue Jesus across the sea.

They are seeking Him.

They want more bread. More signs. More wonders.

But Jesus, never content to give half-truths, speaks of a different kind of hunger. A spiritual hunger. A soul-level emptiness that bread alone cannot touch.

He tells them:

> *"I am the bread of life. Whoever comes to Me shall not hunger, and whoever believes in Me shall never thirst."*
>
> *— John 6:35*

This is no longer metaphor.
This is incarnation language.
The bread of heaven is not a teaching.
It is not a tradition.
It is a Person.
It is the Son of Man Himself.

The Manna That Preceded Him

To the Jewish crowd, bread from heaven would call to mind manna—the miraculous food God gave to their ancestors in the wilderness (Exodus 16). Every morning, they would gather it. Daily. Fresh. Just enough.

But that bread did not give eternal life.
It spoiled by morning.
And everyone who ate it eventually died.
Jesus makes this contrast clear:

> *"Your fathers ate the manna in the wilderness, and they died... I am the living bread that came down from heaven. If anyone eats of this bread, he will live forever."*
>
> *— John 6:49–51*

He is offering not just sustenance, but salvation.
Not just provision, but presence.
Whereas manna came in flakes,
He comes in flesh.

The Flesh of the Son of Man

Then comes the offense.

> *"Truly, truly, I say to you, unless you eat the flesh of the Son of Man and drink His blood, you have no life in you."*

> — *John 6:53*

This was too much for many.
Even His own disciples were shaken.
They said, "This is a hard saying; who can listen to it?"
And yet Jesus does not soften the message.
He presses further, inviting them into the mystery.
What does it mean to eat His flesh?
To drink His blood?
It is not cannibalism.
It is communion.
It is not ritual alone.
It is union with Him—receiving His life into ours,
abiding in Him as nourishment for our very souls.
He is not offering doctrine.
He is offering Himself.

The Offense of Intimacy

Why did this saying cause so many to turn away?
Because it was too personal.
Too raw.
Too physical.
Too inward.
To eat something is to internalize it.
To make it part of you.
Jesus is saying:
You must not just listen to Me. You must receive Me. Deeply. Wholly. Spiritually.
This is not religious performance.
This is divine intimacy.
It means surrender.
It means dependence.
It means letting go of all other sources of life, and saying:
"You, Son of Man, are my only food."

The Role of the Son of Man

It is deliberate that Jesus connects this revelation to His identity as the Son of Man.

> *"The bread that I will give for the life of the world is*
> *My flesh."*

> *— John 6:51*

The Son of Man is the one who comes down from heaven.
Not to judge first, but to give.
Not to demand sacrifice, but to be the sacrifice.
His body is not just a symbol—it is the meal.
And this meal leads to eternal life.
Why "Son of Man"?
Because He comes to identify with our hunger.
Because He descends into our frailty.
Because only a man, touched by hunger, sorrow, and death, can offer life that satisfies forever.

Echoes of the Last Supper

Though John does not record the institution of the Lord's Supper in the same way as the Synoptics, John 6 lays its theological foundation.
When Jesus breaks bread and offers the cup at the Last Supper, He is giving physical expression to what He already proclaimed:

> *"This is My body, given for you... This cup is the new*
> *covenant in My blood."*

> *— Luke 22:19–20*

Communion is not an empty ritual.
It is participation in the mystery of the Son of Man.
Every time we eat that bread,
we proclaim:
He is my life.
He is my nourishment.
He is my eternal sustenance.

The Invitation and the Divide

At the end of John 6, many walk away.
They cannot accept the invitation to eat His flesh, to drink His blood.
And Jesus turns to the twelve and asks:
"Do you also want to go away?"

Peter responds:
"Lord, to whom shall we go? You have the words of eternal life."
This is the dividing line.
Some will seek signs.
Some will demand logic.
Some will walk away.
But those who remain, those who eat, those who receive the Son of Man—they find life.

What It Means for Us
The world is hungry.
And it is starving on junk food—power, entertainment, control, distraction.
But there is only one bread that gives life eternal:
The flesh of the Son of Man.
To receive Him is to be nourished not just in spirit,
but in identity, purpose, joy, and eternity.
He is the bread that comes down from heaven—
not just to fill a belly, but to fill a soul.

Final Reflection
In the desert, God gave manna.
In the upper room, Jesus broke bread.
On the cross, His flesh was torn.
And today, at every table of faith, the Son of Man offers Himself again:

"Take, eat... This is My body."

Not a theory.
Not a doctrine.
But a Person.
He is our bread.
And in Him, we will never hunger again.

CHAPTER 8
The Veil of Flesh
The Son of Man Who Conceals Glory in Humanity

They looked at Him and saw a man.
A man who grew tired.
A man who wept.
A man who bled.
They looked at Him and saw a carpenter,
a son of a poor family from a forgotten town.
They saw hands calloused from labor,
feet dusty from walking,
eyes filled with compassion.
And they missed it.
Because behind that human face,
beneath that fragile flesh,
dwelt the fullness of God.
He was not less than human.
He was more.
He was the veiled glory of God.
And the name He chose to reflect this hiddenness?
Son of Man.

The Hiddenness of God

From the beginning, God has revealed Himself in veils.

- A voice in a burning bush.
- A cloud over a mountain.
- A tabernacle filled with smoke.
- A whisper after the wind.

When Moses asked to see God's glory, God said:

> *"You cannot see My face, for man shall not see Me*
> *and live."*

> — *Exodus 33:20*

So God showed Moses His back, His afterglow—just a glimpse.
Enough to change Moses 'face,
but not enough to destroy him.
God's glory is not safe for the unprepared.
It must be shielded, tempered, veiled.
Which is why the incarnation is not just a miracle—
it is a mercy.
The Son of Man is God made visible—but not overwhelming.
He is fire wrapped in skin,
thunder cloaked in a whisper,
light dimmed to the level of our eyes.

Philippians 2: The Emptying

Paul captures the mystery perfectly:

> *"Though He was in the form of God, He did not*
> *count equality with God a thing to be grasped, but*
> *emptied Himself, taking the form of a servant, being*
> *born in the likeness of men."*

> — *Philippians 2:6–7*

This "emptying" is not the loss of divinity.
It is the laying aside of visible glory.
Jesus does not cease to be God.
He simply refuses to use His divine attributes for His own advantage.
He becomes dependent.
He grows.
He learns.
He suffers.
The One who holds the stars learns how to crawl.
The One who speaks galaxies into being submits to His mother's voice.
This is the veil.
Not a mask.
Not a trick.
But real, full, vulnerable humanity.

Transfiguration: When the Veil Was Lifted

But the glory never left Him.

It was only hidden.

On the Mount of Transfiguration, for a moment, the veil is pulled back:

> *"And He was transfigured before them, and His face*
> *shone like the sun, and His clothes became white as*
> *light."*

> — *Matthew 17:2*

This was not a new glory.

It was the same glory that had always been there—

now revealed.

Peter, James, and John fall on their faces.

The cloud descends.

The voice of the Father speaks:

> *"This is My beloved Son... Listen to Him."*

And then—just as quickly—the veil returns.

Jesus touches them,

and they see no one but Jesus only.

The glory remains hidden again

in the body of the Son of Man.

Isaiah 53: Unremarkable in Appearance

The prophet foresaw this hiddenness:

> *"He had no beauty or majesty to attract us to Him,*
> *nothing in His appearance that we should desire*
> *Him."*

> — *Isaiah 53:2*

He did not come with the grandeur of kings,

nor the glamour of celebrities.

He came as one of us.

And because of that,

most missed Him.

This is the scandal of the incarnation:

That God would come so close, so common, so unnoticed.

That He would hide in plain sight.

The Tabernacle and the Temple

In the wilderness, God's glory dwelt in a tent.
Later, it filled a temple.
Both were outwardly modest.
But inside the veil—behind layers of fabric—was the Most Holy Place.
Where once only priests could enter, and only once a year.
But now?

> *"The Word became flesh and dwelt among us, and*
> *we beheld His glory..."*
>
> *— John 1:14*

The word "dwelt" literally means tabernacled.
Jesus became the new tent.
The new temple.
The new Holy of Holies.
And His flesh was the veil.

The Veil Torn

On the day of His death, as the Son of Man gave up His last breath,
something happened in the temple.

> *"And behold, the veil of the temple was torn in two,*
> *from top to bottom..."*
>
> *— Matthew 27:51*

Why?
Because the true veil—the flesh of Jesus—had been torn.
Access to God was no longer restricted.
The separation between heaven and earth was removed.
The glory that once was hidden is now available.
The Son of Man was not only the veil.
He was the One who opened it forever.

What It Means for Us

We live in a world that worships appearances.
But the Son of Man teaches us:

- That true glory is often hidden.
- That divine power can wear weakness.
- That holiness may look ordinary.

We are not called to be impressive.
We are called to be like Him.
And in us, too, there is glory hidden by grace.
Christ in us—the hope of glory.

Final Reflection

He came wrapped in swaddling cloth.
He lived behind the curtain of flesh.
He spoke softly, walked humbly, wept openly.
But behind it all—was the eternal I AM.
He veiled His glory so we could behold it without being destroyed.
He became like us so we could become like Him.
And now, the veil is torn.
The Son of Man stands—still human, still divine
and invites us to see.
To see beyond the appearance.
To see the glory hidden in the ordinary.
To see God—in flesh, in scars, in mercy.

CHAPTER 9
The Return on the Clouds
The Son of Man Who Comes in Power and Glory

He left in silence.
He will return with sound.
He ascended from a hill—unseen by empires, unrecorded by history books.
But He will descend upon the clouds, and every eye will see Him.
The Son of Man is not finished.
He has walked among us.
He has suffered.
He has died.
He has risen.
But the story is not complete until He comes again.
This is not poetic longing.
This is prophetic certainty.
And when He returns, it will be exactly as He promised—as the Son of Man, riding the clouds of heaven.

Daniel's Vision Fulfilled

We must return to Daniel 7:

> *"I saw in the night visions, and, behold, one like the*
> *Son of Man came with the clouds of heaven... and*
> *there was given Him dominion, and glory, and a*
> *kingdom..." — Daniel 7:13–14*

This vision has not yet reached its fulfillment.
In His first coming, Jesus claimed the identity.
In His second coming, He will display the authority.
He came once to redeem.
He will come again to reign.

Jesus Own Promise

Jesus repeatedly spoke of His return—not vaguely, not symbolically, but with startling clarity.

In the Olivet Discourse, He says:

> *"Then shall appear the sign of the Son of Man in heaven... and they shall see the Son of Man coming in the clouds of heaven with power and great glory."*
>
> *— Matthew 24:30*

Here, Jesus is quoting Daniel—intentionally, prophetically.

He is telling His disciples:

The One Daniel saw? That is Me. I am coming back—on the clouds, with glory, with judgment, with fire.

This return is not spiritual only.

It is not metaphor.

It is literal, visible, final.

And when He comes, the veil is gone forever.

The Testimony of the Angels

At the ascension, as Jesus disappears into the sky, the disciples are left staring upward.

Then two angels appear and say:

> *"This same Jesus, who was taken up from you into heaven, shall so come in like manner as you have seen Him go into heaven."*
>
> *— Acts 1:11*

He left in a body.

He will return in a body.

He left through the sky.

He will return through the sky.

And He will not come quietly.

Revelation's Rider

In Revelation 1:7, John declares:
> *"Behold, He comes with clouds; and every eye shall*
> *see Him..."*

Later, in chapter 19, we see a fuller picture:
> *"And I saw heaven opened, and behold, a white*
> *horse; and He that sat upon him was called Faithful*
> *and True... and on His robe and on His thigh He has*
> *a name written, King of Kings and Lord of Lords."*

This is the Son of Man unveiled.
No longer hidden.
No longer mocked.
No longer betrayed.
But exalted, armed, robed in majesty, and coming to reclaim what is His.

Why the Clouds Matter

In Scripture, clouds are not just weather.
They are symbols of God's presence.

- A cloud led Israel by day.
- A cloud covered Mount Sinai.
- A cloud filled Solomon's temple.
- A cloud enveloped the Mount of Transfiguration.

The cloud is the chariot of divinity.
When Jesus comes on the clouds,
He comes not as a passenger of the skies,
but as the Lord of Heaven—riding the sign of His power.
What Will Happen When He Returns?
Scripture paints the picture:

1. The trumpet will sound.(Thessalonians 4:16)
2. The dead in Christ will rise. The living will be caught up to meet Him. The nations will mourn. (Matthew 24:30)
3. He will judge in righteousness.(Revelation 20)
4. He will establish a new heaven and a new earth.

This is not a return to improve the world—It is a return to remake it.
The King will come.
The kingdom will be visible.
And the Son of Man will reign forever.

No One Knows the Day

Jesus also says:

> *"But of that day and hour knows no man... but My Father only."*

> — *Matthew 24:36*

This is not a puzzle to solve.
It is a call to readiness.
We are not meant to calculate His return.
We are meant to prepare for it.
And those who are watching, waiting, and faithful
will not be surprised.

The Son of Man as the Returning King

He came once riding a donkey.
He will come again riding the clouds.
He came once in humility.
He will come again in glory.
He came once to be judged.
He will come again as the Judge.
And every knee will bow.
Every tongue will confess.
Not by compulsion, but by revelation.
They will see Him as He is—not just a man,
but the Son of Man in power.

What It Means for Us

The return of the Son of Man is not a threat—it is a promise.
It means:

- Justice is coming.
  Evil will not have the final word.
- Resurrection is coming.
  Death will not win.
- Glory is coming.

The veiled Jesus will be seen.
And those who are His—
who trusted Him in sorrow,
who followed Him in weakness,
who waited through the dark—they will rejoice.

Because the clouds will part.
And the Son of Man will return.
Not as a memory.
Not as a myth.
But as a King.

Final Reflection

Look to the sky.
Not in superstition.
But in hope.
Live each day as though the clouds might break.
Live each moment as though the King is watching.
Because one day—soon—He will come.
And when He does, we will say with joy:
> *"Behold, this is our God; we have waited for Him."*

> *— Isaiah 25:9*

The Son of Man is coming again.
And this time,
every eye will see Him.

CHAPTER 10
Dominion Restored
The Son of Man Who Reclaims What Was Lost

In Eden, a crown was placed upon humanity.
A dominion not earned, but gifted.
God said,

"Let them have dominion..."

Genesis 1:26

Over the earth. Over the animals. Over creation itself.
But that crown slipped.
That dominion was forfeited—
not stolen by an enemy stronger,
but surrendered through disobedience.
Adam traded kingship for shame.
Eve traded inheritance for exile.
The world that was once subject to man
now groans under the weight of sin.
But the story does not end in the garden.
A Second Adam would come.
One who would not fall.
One who would reclaim what was lost.
One who would wear the crown rightly.
That One... is the Son of Man.

From Dust to Dominion

Psalm 8 gives us a riddle:

> *"What is man, that Thou art mindful of him? And
> the son of man, that Thou visitest him? For Thou
> hast made him a little lower than the angels, and
> hast crowned him with glory and honour. Thou
> madest him to have dominion over the works of Thy
> hands..."*

> *— Psalm 8:4–6*

David speaks of mankind—created in humility, destined for glory.
But Hebrews 2 interprets this psalm Christologically:

> *"But we see Jesus, who was made a little lower than
> the angels... crowned with glory and honour... that
> He by the grace of God should taste death for every
> man."*

> *— Hebrews 2:9*

In other words:
Psalm 8 is ultimately about Jesus.
He is the true Son of Man—
not just in title, but in function.
The One who fulfills the lost destiny of humanity.

Adam Failed — Yeshua Fulfilled

- Adam was placed in a garden.
  Yeshua entered a wilderness.
- Adam was tempted and fell.
  Yeshua was tempted and stood.
- Adam chose his will over God's.
  Yeshua chose God's will over His own:
  > *"Not My will, but Thine be done."*

  > *— Luke 22:42*

- Adam's disobedience brought death.
- Yeshua's obedience brought life.
  Through Adam, dominion was lost.
- Through Yeshua, dominion is restored.

This is not poetic symmetry.
This is the spine of salvation history.
The first man was of the earth, earthy.
The Second Man is the Lord from heaven. (1 Corinthians 15:47)
The Son of Man restores the reign.

Authority Declared

After the resurrection, Yeshua says:

> *"All authority in heaven and on earth has been
> given to Me."*
>
> *— Matthew 28:18*

This is not symbolic authority.
It is actual dominion—over heaven and earth.
He has received what Adam lost.
He now holds the keys of death and hell (Revelation 1:18).
He is enthroned—not in theory, but in reality.
We do not await His kingship.
We await its full manifestation.
The kingdom is already.
The kingdom is also coming.

Seated at the Right Hand

In Daniel 7, the Son of Man is brought before the Ancient of Days.
He receives a kingdom.
In Psalm 110, David writes:

> *"The Lord said unto my Lord, Sit at My right hand,
> until I make Thine enemies Thy footstool."*

Jesus quoted this verse to His critics.
And after the resurrection, He fulfilled it.
He sat down at the right hand of God.
Not because His work was over entirely—but because His sacrifice was complete, and His authority was confirmed.
The Son of Man now reigns.

Dominion Shared

But here is the great mystery:

He doesn't reign alone.

He shares His dominion with us.

"If we suffer with Him, we shall also reign with Him."

— 2 Timothy 2:12

"To him that overcomes will I grant to sit with Me in My throne…"

— Revelation 3:21

We, who were slaves to sin, are now heirs with Christ.

The Son of Man restores not only His own throne—but ours.

We are made kings and priests.

We are given new authority.

We walk in power not our own.

Because He reigns, we reign.

Because He conquered, we overcome.

The Kingdom Without End

The Son of Man's dominion is not temporary.

"His dominion is an everlasting dominion, which shall not pass away, and His kingdom one that shall not be destroyed."

— Daniel 7:14

This dominion:

- Cannot be corrupted.
- Cannot be voted out.
- Cannot be overthrown.

It is not fragile.

It is not democratic.

It is divine.

It is not merely over souls.

It is over everything:

Time, space, history, matter, angels, and nations.

This is why He is called King of kings and Lord of lords.

What It Means for Us

We were made to rule—not in pride, but in purpose.
To walk in dominion over sin, over fear, over death.
The Son of Man restores our authority.
Not by exalting us, but by lifting us with Him.
We do not claim crowns by conquest, but by union with Christ.
And every step we take in obedience is a step back into the dominion for which we were made.

Final Reflection

In the end, the Son of Man is not just a title.
It is a mission.
He came to reclaim the image of God in man.
He came to restore what was lost.
He came to give back the crown.
And He succeeded.
Now He reigns.
And because He reigns, so shall we.
The throne that was once empty is now occupied.
Not by an angel.
Not by a tyrant.
But by a man—The Son of Man.
And in Him, humanity is restored to its rightful place.

> *"Every eye shall see Him — the Son of Man*
> *returning on the clouds with great glory."*

> *— Matthew 24:30*

> *"Behold, He cometh with clouds; and every eye shall*
> *see Him..."*

> *— Revelation 1:7*

CLOUDS OF HEAVEN
THE RETURN OF THE SON OF MAN

Damiano B. Centola

CHAPTER 11
The Suffering Son of Man
The Wounds That Prove His Glory

He could have come with a sword.
He came with scars.
He could have ruled from Caesar's throne.
He chose a cross of wood.
He could have summoned twelve legions of angels.
Instead, He walked alone.
The Son of Man was not only destined for dominion.
He was destined for suffering.
This, above all, is the scandal and glory of the Gospel—that God came
down not only to reign, but to bleed.
And it is through this suffering that His kingship is sealed,
His mercy unveiled,
and our salvation purchased.

A Paradox Foretold

The Jews of Jesus 'day were not wrong to expect a conquering Messiah.
The Son of Man was to receive dominion and glory and a kingdom
(Daniel 7:14).
But they missed the mystery:
The path to the throne runs through the grave.
The prophets had seen it—dimly, painfully:

> *"He is despised and rejected of men; a Man of*
> *sorrows, and acquainted with grief... He was*
> *wounded for our transgressions..."*

> *— Isaiah 53:3-5*

This is not a description of a royal warrior.
This is the vision of a suffering servant.

And yet Jesus calls Himself "the Son of Man" more than any other name.

By doing so, He links the exalted Danielic figure with the Isaian Servant.

He says, I am both.

Crowned and crushed.

Exalted and executed.

Glorious and grief-stricken.

The Prophecy in His Mouth

Jesus speaks of His suffering not as an accident,
but as His assignment.

> *"The Son of Man must suffer many things, and be rejected... and be killed, and after three days rise again."*
>
> *— Mark 8:31*

Here He unites the two great visions:

- Daniel's Son of Man: who comes in clouds.
- Isaiah's Suffering Servant: who is pierced for our iniquities.

And He tells us:

They are one and the same.

No one took His life.

He laid it down.

No one defeated Him.

He submitted—for our sake.

The Garden and the Cup

In Gethsemane, we see the cost of the Son of Man's mission.

> *"My soul is exceeding sorrowful, even unto death...*
> *Father, if it be possible, let this cup pass from Me..."*
>
> *— Matthew 26:38–39*

This is not weakness.

This is holy agony.

He, who created the universe,

now trembles before the wrath of sin's judgment.

And still He says:

> *"Nevertheless, not as I will, but as Thou wilt."*

The Son of Man surrenders.
Not to Rome.
Not to Satan.
But to the Father.
Betrayed and Condemned
He is betrayed by a kiss.
Tried by liars.
Mocked by soldiers.
Spit upon by the ones He came to save.
And when the high priest demands clarity:
> *"Tell us if You are the Christ, the Son of God."*

Jesus responds:
> *"You will see the Son of Man sitting at the right hand of Power, and coming with the clouds of heaven."*

> *— Matthew 26:64*

He speaks Daniel 7 in the face of death.
And they tear their garments.
Because He dared to say: The Son of Man is Me.

The Cross and the Cry

And so He is crucified.
Between thieves.
Exposed, beaten, shamed.
Yet even here, He speaks as the Son of Man.
"Father, forgive them."
"Today you will be with Me in Paradise."
"It is finished."
These are not the words of a victim.
They are the words of a King dying for His kingdom.
In John 3:14, Jesus had said:
> *"As Moses lifted up the serpent in the wilderness, even so must the Son of Man be lifted up..."*

And now He is.
Lifted on wood.
Hung between heaven and earth.
The bridge between the holy and the fallen.
The Son of Man suffers.
And in doing so, He saves.

The Tomb and the Silence

He is wrapped in linen.
Laid in a borrowed grave.
The earth that He made now holds His body.
And for three days, the world is still.
But heaven is not.
For the Son of Man had promised:

> *"...and after three days, rise again."*

And when He rises,
He rises not just as a survivor, but as a conqueror.

The Scars Remain

Even after the resurrection, the Son of Man retains His wounds.

> *"Reach here your finger... see My hands. Put your hand into My side..."*
>
> *— John 20:27*

He does not hide them.
He does not erase them.
Why?
Because they are the proof of love, the mark of victory,
the crown of suffering.

> *In heaven, the One on the throne is called "a Lamb as it had been slain."*
>
> *— Revelation 5:6*

This is the eternal paradox:
The Son of Man rules by suffering.

What It Means for Us

We serve a King who knows pain.

A Savior who did not bypass the cross.

A God who entered our weakness, tasted our tears, and bore our shame.

Because He suffered:

- We are healed.
- We are forgiven.
- We are made whole.

And now, when we suffer, we are not abandoned.

We follow a Lord who has walked this path before.

Final Reflection

The Son of Man could have come in fire.

He came in flesh.

He could have sat upon a throne.

He chose a cross.

He could have demanded sacrifice.

He became the sacrifice.

And that, beloved, is why He is worthy of all glory.

His suffering is.

CHAPTER 12
The Son of Man and the Final Judgment
When Mercy Sits on the Throne

The first time He came, He came riding a donkey.
The next time, He will come on the clouds.
The first time, He came to be judged.
The next time, He will be the Judge.
The Son of Man, once mocked and crucified,
will return with glory, authority, and the books of eternity.
And every knee will bow—not out of coercion, but because truth will
stand visible, and every soul will know.
He who bore our sins
will now weigh our lives.
He who wept for the lost
will now separate the saved from the condemned.
This is not myth.
This is not metaphor.
This is the unfolding reality of the Gospel.

A Throne of Glory

Jesus spoke of this moment with precision:

> *"When the Son of Man shall come in His glory, and*
> *all the holy angels with Him, then shall He sit upon*
> *the throne of His glory..."*

> — *Matthew 25:31*

This throne is not David's earthly seat.
It is not the Sanhedrin's seat of judgment.
It is the eternal throne,
prepared from the foundation of the world.
And upon it sits a Man.
Not an angel.
Not a myth.
Not a force.
The Son of Man—Yeshua,
flesh and glory, scars and light.
He will not come silently this time.
He will not be misunderstood.
He will not be rejected.
He will be recognized by every soul.

The Gathering of Nations

Jesus continues:

> *"Before Him shall be gathered all nations: and He*
> *shall separate them one from another, as a*
> *shepherd divides his sheep from the goats."*
>
> *— Matthew 25:32*

This is the global moment.
The universal reckoning.
The curtain call of history.
Not just Israel.
Not just the Church.
Not just Rome or Babylon or the West.
All nations.
Every tribe.
Every language.
Every people.
All will stand before the One they crucified.
And truth will be the only language spoken.

The Criteria of the King

Many expect thunder.
But Jesus gives wheat and water.

> *"I was hungry, and you gave Me meat. I was thirsty,*
> *and you gave Me drink. I was a stranger, and you*
> *took Me in..."*
>
> *— Matthew 25:35*

And the righteous answer:
"When did we see You?"
They did not know they were feeding the King.
But in serving the least, they had honored the Lord.

> *"Inasmuch as you have done it unto one of the least*
> *of these My brethren, you have done it unto Me."*

This is the judgment of love.
A weighing not of perfection, but of compassion.
The goats?
They ignored the broken, and by doing so, ignored the Christ.
Their judgment is not arbitrary.
It is revealing.
What they did not do exposed who they truly were.

Justice and Righteousness

The Son of Man does not judge on rumor.
He does not base His verdict on appearance.

> *"He shall not judge after the sight of His eyes,*
> *neither reprove after the hearing of His ears: but*
> *with righteousness shall He judge the poor..."*
>
> *— Isaiah 11:3–4*

This Judge sees everything.
Not only our actions, but our motives.
Not only our deeds, but our silence.
He sees the unspoken bitterness.
He sees the private mercy.
He judges in perfect truth, and no lie can hide from His eyes.

The Books Are Opened

John saw it in Revelation:

*"And I saw a great white throne... and the dead
were judged out of those things which were written
in the books, according to their works."*

— Revelation 20:12

The books of deeds are opened.

And then, the Book of Life.

Those whose names are found written in the Lamb's Book of Life enter into eternal rest.

Those who rejected the Son of Man face eternal separation.

This is not vengeance.

This is the final, irreversible unveiling of justice.

Mercy has spoken for centuries.

Grace has been offered in every generation.

But now, the time of reaping has come.

The Final Word Is His

*"e has given Him authority to execute judgment
also, because He is the Son of Man."*

— John 5:27

Why the Son of Man?

Why not the Father?

Why not the Spirit?

Because only a Man can judge men.

Only the One who was tempted, yet without sin.

Only the One who wept, hungered, suffered, died, and rose.

His judgment is righteous because it is personal.

He knows what it means to be human.

He bore our dust and our burdens.

And so when He judges, He does so with perfect equity.

What It Means for Us

- If you are in Christ, you need not fear the judgment.
- The Judge is your Advocate.

The Son of Man has already taken your sentence.

- If you are outside of Him, then today is the day of salvation.

He still stands with open arms, scars visible, inviting you to come home. But the day will come when He closes the scroll, and all accounts are finalized.

Final Reflection

The Son of Man came first with mercy in His hands.

He will return with justice on His lips.

He who stood silent before Pilate will now call all kings to account.

He who forgave the thief will now examine every heart.

The throne will not be empty.

The Judge will not be blind.

The verdict will not be delayed.

And the Son of Man—pierced, risen, glorified—will speak the final word over every soul.

Let us live now as those who will see His face.

Let us love now as those who will be measured by mercy.

Let us worship now as those whose names are written in the Lamb's Book of Life.

CHAPTER 13
The Glory Revealed in a
Human Face Behold, the Man

The universe has never been more radiant than the moment when God's glory took on a human face.
Not in the splitting of the Red Sea, nor the fire atop Sinai,
nor the vision of wheels within wheels—but in the eyes of a carpenter, in the calloused hands of a rabbi, in the tears of a man kneeling in Gethsemane.
"Behold, the Man."
Pilate said it mockingly.
He had no idea he was announcing the mystery of all mysteries:
The invisible God made visible.
The eternal Word made flesh.
The glory of heaven walking among us.
And we beheld Him—not just as a teacher or prophet, but as the embodiment of divine beauty, majesty, and mercy.

The Face That Shone Before the World Was Made

Long before Bethlehem,
before Adam, before light pierced the darkness—the Son existed.
> *"He is the brightness of His glory, and the express*
> *image of His person..."*

> *— Hebrews 1:3*

This is not poetic exaggeration.
This is theology at its most profound.
The Son of Man is not just anointed.
He is glory itself in bodily form.
Moses once asked to see God's glory.
God said, "You cannot see My face and live."

But now—through Jesus—we do.

The Tabernacle of Flesh

John writes:

> *"And the Word was made flesh, and dwelt among*
> *us, and we beheld His glory..."*

> *— John 1:14*

The Greek word for "dwelt" here means tabernacled.

As God's presence once filled the tent in the wilderness,
now His fullness dwells in a man.

But not just any man.

The Son of Man.

- Not remote like thunder.
- Not concealed like smoke.
- Not distant like law.

But near, touchable, knowable, embraceable.

The glory of God now walked in sandals, slept under stars, and looked
into human eyes with eternal compassion.

The Eyes of the Redeemer

To see His face was to see:

- Truth without pretense
- Power without pride
- Mercy without measure

What did the leper see when Jesus touched him?

What did Peter see when He turned and looked at him after
the denial?

What did Mary see when He called her name outside the tomb?

Those weren't just moments of human connection.

They were encounters with God's face unveiled.

> *"In Your face, O Lord, will I seek."*

> *— Psalm 27:8*

Now that face had a name. **Yeshua.**

Transfigured on the Mountain

There was one moment when the veil briefly lifted:

> *"His face did shine as the sun, and His raiment was*
> *white as the light..."*

> *— Matthew 17:2*

On the mount of Transfiguration, three disciples beheld the radiance of unfiltered glory.

He had always been divine—but now they saw it.

Not light reflected.

Light emanated.

The Son of Man shone with the brilliance of heaven, yet still bore the tenderness of earth.

Moses and Elijah stood beside Him.

But only Jesus remained.

The Law and the Prophets had served their time.

Now the Face of God would speak.

> *"This is My beloved Son... hear Him."*

The Face That Was Struck

And yet, this glorious face was spat upon.

Slapped.

Bruised.

Beard torn.

> *"They shall smite the judge of Israel with a rod*
> *upon the cheek."*
>
> *— Micah 5:1*

The One who smiled at children was now disfigured by hatred.

And yet, He did not turn away.

> *"I gave My back to the smiters... and My face I did*
> *not hide from shame and spitting."*
>
> *— Isaiah 50:6*

He let His face be defiled
so that ours could be redeemed.

Recognized in the Breaking of Bread

After the resurrection, His followers did not immediately recognize Him.
But in one sacred moment:

> *"He took bread, blessed and broke it... and their*
> *eyes were opened, and they knew Him."*

> — *Luke 24:30–31*

Not through thunder.
Not through vision.
But through fellowship.
They recognized Him in the simplicity of bread and presence.
The Son of Man's glory is often hidden in the humble.

The Face in the Clouds

He will return again.
And this time, no one will miss it.

> *"They shall see the Son of Man coming in the clouds*
> *of heaven with power and great glory."*

> — *Matthew 24:30*

And John tells us:

> *"His face was as the sun shines in its strength..."*

> — *Revelation 1:16*

This is not the face of the beaten prisoner.
This is the face of the eternal King, The Alpha and Omega.
The One whose eyes are as fire and whose voice is as many waters.
And still—He bears the scars.
Not erased, but glorified.

What It Means for Us

- We were created to behold God's face.

Sin turned us away.

Jesus turns us back.

- In the face of Jesus, we see not only who God is—but who we were meant to be.
- When we look to Him, we are changed from glory to glory.
  "The light of the knowledge of the glory of God in
  the face of Jesus Christ."

— 2 Corinthians 4:6

And one day—we will see Him face to face.

And we shall be like Him.

Final Reflection

The Son of Man came not in fire, but in flesh.

He carried the weight of eternal glory in a fragile human frame.

And He allowed that frame to be broken—so that ours could
be healed.

One day, when the clouds' part, and the trumpet sounds, we will see His
face.

Not as Pilate did.

Not as the Pharisees did.

Not as a criminal.

But as a Bridegroom, a King, a Redeemer, a Brother, a God.

The face we were always meant to see—the face that changes everything.

CHAPTER 14
The Son of Man in Us Glory Reflected Through Dust

There is a mystery not just in who Yeshua is—but in what He came to do through us.

If the Son of Man is the perfect union of divinity and dust, then His mission does not end at the cross or the empty tomb.

It continues in us.

We are not mere spectators of His glory.

We are the mirrors through which it shines.

He, the Son of Man, took on our form so that we might take on His nature.

And now—through grace, through obedience, and through the indwelling of the Holy Spirit—His glory lives again…in vessels of clay.

The Original Intention: Glory in Dust

> *"Then the Lord God formed man of the dust of the*
> *ground, and breathed into his nostrils the breath of*
> *life; and man became a living soul."*

> *— Genesis 2:7*

From the very beginning, dust was never meant to remain just dust.

When animated by the breath of God, it became the image-bearer of the Eternal.

Yet something was broken.

The mirror shattered.

The reflection distorted.

Sin reduced glory to shame.

Dust returned to dust.

But in Jesus—the true Son of Man—we see the restoration of that original purpose.

He was not made of celestial metal or divine mist.

He was born into human frailty, not to remain in it,
but to transform it.

The Incarnation Continues

The early Church said something profound:

> *"God became man so that man might become
> godlike."*
>
> *— Athanasius, 4th century*

They did not mean we become God.
But that we are meant to share in His likeness, just as Adam once did—
now, through Christ, in a new and living way.
Paul echoes this in his letter to the Corinthians:

> *"But we all, with open face beholding as in a glass
> the glory of the Lord, are changed into the same
> image from glory to glory, even as by the Spirit of
> the Lord."*
>
> *— 2 Corinthians 3:18*

We behold His glory, and in beholding, we are transformed.
The Son of Man did not come merely to reveal glory—He came to
replicate it.

The Spirit of the Son

When Jesus ascended, He did not abandon us.

> *"I will not leave you comfortless: I will come to
> you."*
>
> *— John 14:18*

He breathed on His disciples.
He sent the Holy Spirit.
And what did Paul later call this Spirit?

> *"God hath sent forth the Spirit of His Son into your
> hearts, crying, Abba, Father."*
>
> *— Galatians 4:6*

The Spirit of the Son of Man now lives in us.
It is this Spirit that cries out not only "Father,"
but also teaches us how to live like the Son—to walk in obedience, to suffer with joy, to serve with humility, to radiate divine light from within dust-formed vessels.

Vessels of Earth, Filled with Heaven

"We have this treasure in earthen vessels, that the excellency of the power may be of God, and not of us."

— 2 Corinthians 4:7

The mystery of the Gospel is not just that God came down—but that He now dwells within.
Through faith in Jesus, we become carriers of glory.
Not by might.
Not by intellect.
But by mercy.

- The Son of Man now shines through:
- The widow who still prays in pain
- The child who forgives without understanding
- The prisoner who sings in the darkness
- The martyr who smiles as the sword is lifted

Glory does not avoid suffering.
It transfigures it.

He Will Be Seen in Us

In Revelation, John sees not only Jesus in His glorified state—
but he also sees the Church, clothed in white, radiant, victorious.
We are not just the redeemed.
We are the reflected.
When the Son of Man returns, He will recognize Himself in those who are His.
Not because of our titles.
Not because of our wealth.

But because our lives mirror His.

- His humility in our service
- His purity in our thoughts
- His courage in our witness
- His love in our forgiveness

The early believers were called "Christians"—little Christs—because people saw Him in them.

The mission has not changed.

The Face of Glory Now

We no longer see Him face to face.
But we are called to be His face.

"As the Father hath sent Me, even so send I you."

— John 20:21

The Son of Man was sent to dwell among us.
Now we are sent to dwell among others in the same way.
To eat with sinners.
To kneel beside the broken.
To weep with those who mourn.
To preach good news to the poor.
And above all, to embody the nearness of God.

The Secret Glory in Ordinary Saints

The world expects glory to shout.
But the Son of Man whispers.
He hides glory in places we overlook:

- A mother who prays unseen
- A worker who gives thanks in silence
- A man who turns the other cheek without applause

These are icons of the invisible.

They are proof that the Son of Man is still moving,
still transforming,
still shining.

We Shall Be Like Him

*"Beloved, now are we the sons of God, and it doth
not yet appear what we shall be: but we know that,
when He shall appear, we shall be like Him;*

for we shall see Him as He is."

— 1 John 3:2

The Son of Man became like us, so that we could become like Him.
And though now we wrestle with weakness, though our dust sometimes
clouds His light—a day is coming.
We will shine.
Not with borrowed radiance.
But with the full light of His glory in us.

Final Reflection

Yeshua did not only come to save us.
He came to inhabit us.
To take dust and breathe glory into it again.
To make of us what we were always meant to be:
mirrors of heaven, sons of light, flesh filled with fire.
The Son of Man walks the earth still.
Look closely.
He walks through you.

CHAPTER 15
Epilogue: When the Son of Man Stands

It began in vision.
A prophet far from his homeland saw a throne ablaze, a courtroom of heaven, and One "like the Son of Man" approaching the Ancient of Days, surrounded by clouds.
It ends in glory.
But not the kind the world understands.
Not the fleeting flare of empires or the roar of earthly thrones.
No—this is a glory that rises silently.
A glory that cannot die.
A glory that stands.

The Final Scene

> *"Behold, He cometh with clouds; and every eye shall see Him..."*
>
> *— Revelation 1:7*

He came once, unnoticed by kings, born in a feeding trough, raised in obscurity, crucified between thieves.
But He will not return unnoticed.
The same clouds that carried Him away will carry Him back.
And this time, He will stand.

The Standing King

The Scriptures say He sat down at the right hand of the Father (Hebrews 10:12).
His work was finished.
The cross had spoken.
The tomb had opened.
He took His place.

But there is one moment in the New Testament when the Son of Man does not sit.

When Stephen, the first martyr, was about to die, he looked up and declared:

"Behold, I see the heavens opened,

and the Son of Man standing at the right hand of God."

— Acts 7:56

Why standing?
Not for judgment.
Not for spectacle.
But to receive one of His own.
To honor the one who bore His likeness.
To stand for the one who stood for Him.
This is not just a gesture.
It is a promise.

When He Stands Again

A day is coming—not of vision, but of reality—when the Son of Man will rise from His throne to judge the living and the dead.

"When the Son of Man shall come in His glory,

and all the holy angels with Him,

then shall He sit upon the throne of His glory."

— Matthew 25:31

He will separate light from darkness.
Truth from deception.
Those who knew Him from those who only used His name.
He will stand not only as Judge—but as Justifier, Redeemer, Bridegroom, King.

The Wounds Still Show

When Thomas doubted, Jesus appeared and said:

"Reach hither thy finger, and behold My hands."

— John 20:27

The Son of Man did not shed His scars after resurrection.
He kept them.

And He keeps them still.
When He returns, the signs of His suffering will remain.
Not as reminders of pain—but as eternal receipts of love paid in full.
The Judge bears wounds.
The King still bleeds.
The Glory still remembers dust.

Every Eye Shall See

"And then shall appear the sign of the Son of Man in heaven...

and they shall see the Son of Man coming in the clouds of heaven with power and great glory."

— Matthew 24:30

He will not be hidden.
Not this time.
The nations will mourn.
The proud will tremble.
The broken will rise.
The faithful will rejoice.
And those who knew His voice in secret
will recognize Him in glory.

A Mirror Fully Restored

"For now we see through a glass, darkly;

but then face to face..."

— 1 Corinthians 13:12

The Son of Man has been restoring the mirror—the human soul fractured by sin—one shard at a time.
On that day, when He stands again in glory, the mirror will be whole.
And we will not only see Him.
We will be like Him.

The Final Breath

He called Himself "Son of Man"
more than any other title.
Not Rabbi.
Not Prophet.
Not even Messiah.
Because He came not only to rule us—but to reach us.
Not only to redeem our souls—but to inhabit our lives.
He walked where we walk.
He wept where we weep.
He died the death we fear.
And He rose with the life we could never earn.
Now He waits.
Now He watches.
Now He intercedes.
But soon—the Son of Man will stand once more.
And the heavens will open.
And the nations will fall silent.
And the stars will realign.
And time itself will bow.
And every tongue shall confess:
This is the Son of Man—the Glory hidden in flesh, the Fire wrapped in dust, the Mirror of God restored.

Hic est Filius Hominis—Gloria in carne abscondita,

Ignis pulvere tectus,Speculum Dei restitutum.

—D.B.C.

THE FACE OF DUST AND GLORY

Damiano B. Centola

ACKNOWLEDGMENTS

I offer all glory to the Most High—the Ancient of Days who sent His
Son clothed in dust, so that we might be clothed in glory.

To my beloved wife, Feebe—your unwavering love, spiritual
discernment, and prophetic sensitivity helped shape the very spirit of this
work.

You continue to walk with me on every holy hill and through every
sacred page.

To my Pop—seer, thinker, and witness to the mysteries of God.

You taught me to tremble before truth.

To every reader who has walked with me through the mystery of the Son
of Man—may your heart be set ablaze with wonder, and your life reflect
His image.

And to the One who still bears the scars—who sits at the right hand of
Majesty, and yet still walks beside us as the Son of Man this book is
Yours.

Other Books by Damiano B. Centola

1. Mother of Corruption: Unveiling Spiritual Corruption from Babylon to Today
2. God's Sovereignty: Exploring the Divine Rule Over Creation, History, and Eternity
3. Divine Encounters: Discovering the Depth and Power of God's Names
4. The Lord is My Shepherd: A Journey Through Psalm 23
5. I Choose the Call: My Daily Anthem of Devotion
6. The Mystery of Mysteries: Decoding the Divine Proportions of the Human Body Through Art, Anatomy, and Sacred Geometry
7. Jewish Holidays: Jesus Teaches Us Through Sacred Seasons
8. The Words of Jesus: Unlocking the Lord's Prayer in Aramaic, Greek, and English
9. YESHUA (יֵשׁוּעַ): The Nazarene, the Refugee, the Redeemer
10. Yeshua the Builder: From Bethlehem to the Baptism
11. The Bread of Life: A Journey to Bethlehem
12. Water Jar: Devotions from the Shadows of Scripture
13. The Mountain Still Speaks, Volume I: Salt, Light, and Fire from the Sermon That Changed the World
14. The Mountain Still Speaks, Volume II: Still He Speaks — Echoes from the Higher Ground, the Narrow Way, the Secret Life, and the Rock That Stands
15. Son of Man: The Glory Hidden in Flesh
16. Five Pillars (forthcoming)

REFERENCES & SOURCE CITATIONS

All Scripture quotations are taken from the King James Version (KJV) of the Holy Bible unless otherwise noted.

Primary Biblical References:

- Daniel 7:13–14 – The Son of Man comes with clouds before the Ancient of Days
- Psalm 8:4–6 –"What is man… crowned with glory and honour"
- Ezekiel 2:1 " –Son of man, stand upon thy feet…"
- Matthew 24:30, 25:31–32, 26:64 – Return and final judgment of the Son of Man
- Mark 8:31, 10:45, 14:62 – Suffering, ransom, and identity of the Son of Man
- Luke 17:21, 22:69 – The Kingdom within and the Son of Man enthroned
- John 1:51, 3:14–15, 6:53, 20:27 – The ladder, lifted-up serpent, bread of life, and risen Christ
- Acts 7:56 – Stephen sees the Son of Man standing
- Revelation 1:13–18, 14:14, 19:11–16 – Son of Man crowned in glory and judgment
- Hebrews 4:15, 10:12 – High Priest, seated after atonement
- 1 Corinthians 13:12 – We shall see face to face

Secondary Sources and Theological Concepts:

- Theological Wordbook of the Old Testament – G.K. Keil & Ludwig Koehler
- The New International Dictionary of New Testament Theology – Colin Brown (Editor)
- The Book of Mysteries – Jonathan Cahn (for poetic framing, not theology)
- Church Fathers and Apostolic Writings – Ignatius of Antioch, Irenaeus
- Strong's Concordance and Lexicon – For Hebrew and Greek word studies
- Hebrew and Aramaic transliterations verified through Sefaria and STEP Bible tool

ABOUT THE AUTHOR

Damiano B. Centola is a passionate author and devoted student of God's Word. With a heart for teaching and a gift for connecting biblical truths to modern life, Damiano has authored several works that inspire spiritual growth and deeper faith. Through a blend of theological insight and personal reflection, his writings encourage readers to encounter God in transformative ways. Damiano resides in Los Angeles with his family, pursuing a life of faith, service, and creativity.

www.ingramcontent.com/pod-product-compliance
Lightning Source LLC
Chambersburg PA
CBHW051224120626
46547CB00013B/1492